POCKET IMA(

Lytham St Anne's

Lytham St Anne's Lifeboat Monument.

POCKET IMAGES

Lytham St Anne's

Catherine Rothwell

NONSUCH

First published 1993
This new pocket edition 2007
Images unchanged from first edition

Nonsuch Publishing Limited
Cirencester Road, Chalford
Stroud, Gloucestershire, GL6 8PE
www.nonsuch-publishing.com

Nonsuch Publishing is an imprint of NPI Media Group

British Library Cataloguing in Publication Data.
A catalogue record for this book is available from the British Library.

ISBN 978-1-84588-423-9

Typesetting and origination by NPI Media Group
Printed in Great Britain

Contents

Introduction

Some towns more than others instil in the sensitive traveller a feeling of walking in the footsteps of past generations. Such a town is Lytham St Anne's, and it is good that early visitors to this now renowned resort left behind memories and impressions with which we can identify today. Mr Whittle of Preston, who came in 1824, reported in *Marina* that he had watched the Lardner troupe of comedians performing at the New Theatre, Lytham. Seemingly straight out of a Charles Dickens novel, this enterprising family not only scintillated in the farce *The Irish Tutor or New Lights*, but they also 'took likenesses', an expression my photographer father was still using in the 1920s, while child prodigy Master Lardner taught dancing between performances.

The population of Lytham in the 1820s was 1,292 and the clay and straw of a primitive civilization was fast being replaced with good building brick and stone. One of a line of charismatic and generous squires, John Clifton laid out a racecourse of three miles circuit, with paddocks, stables and a string of fine bloodstock; one, Lizmahago, gave its name to the group of white cottages erected for visitors. William Hornby of Kirkham built a Chinese marine residence for his summer use, and in 1845 Philip Ryecroft of South Shore wanted clay 'for the grand Marine Drive between South Shore and Blackpool', an extension of Clifton Drive begun by the squire of Lytham Hall. The name of the daily coach, *Enterprise*, summed up the entrepreneurial spirit in the town as more visitors arrived.

The lives of the Clifton family, seemingly imbued with wealth and wanderlust, make colourful reading. John Talbot Clifton, fresh from big game hunting and having just recovered from 'black fever' contracted in Uganda, determined to witness the final stages of the South African campaign (the Boer War) and set his yacht accordingly. Perhaps the sea air bred a questing spirit in the mid-nineteenth century, as Charles Maries, an organist at St Anne's church, left his post to seek rare plants in China and Japan.

A scheme to cut a canal from Preston to Lytham, accommodating vessels of up to 250 tons and thus eliminating the need for seagoing lighters, might have made 1833 an *annus mirabilis*, but even though the eighteen directors had Mr Clifton's financial backing the scheme came to naught. Captain Rymer's *Mary and Ann* continued to take sacks of flour and oats by sea to Preston, while Captain Fell's *Thomas and Mary* brought cargoes of barley from Carlisle to Lytham Pool.

Such futuristic schemes were hatched when ancient customs still died hard. Bull baiting was still carried on close to the fish stones and the public oven in Market Square. This barbarous sport tenderized the meat before the animal's slaughter and was not banned until William IV's reign. In those days of few shops the parson, after the service at St Cuthbert's, would announce, 'Farmer Cookson will kill a cow on Tuesday. Anyone wanting to buy meat may get it on the day following.' The same churchman also instructed the bellman or town crier to call out on Saturday night, 'Once more dark and then Sunday', as a reminder for all to come to church.

Old inhabitants recalled with glee salty characters from the days of the Improvement Commissioners and, more recently, the Urban District Council. One of these was the much-loved teetotaller John Myerscough whose misuse of the Queen's English led to great hilarity. 'If this argument goes on any longer,' he once said, 'I shall vaccinate my seat.'

News of stirring national events filtered through the mundane pattern of local life in Lytham: General Gordon at Khartoum; the Relief of Mafeking; the visit of Shackleton to King Edward VII School to lecture on his quest for the South Pole; Paulhan flying at Squire's Gate in 1909 ('our man, Grahame-Whyte could not get off the ground'); the stunned impression of horrified disbelief left by the sinking of the *Titanic*; and the continuing tragedy of the First World War.

By the end of the nineteenth century a marvellous change had spread over neighbouring St Anne's-on-Sea. Shippons (cowsheds), slaughterhouses, stables and whitewashed cottages had all disappeared, and where there were once bare, green fields there were now wide, clean streets, fine shops and houses. The population swelled to 15,000. Whereas in 1873 the only meeting place for entertainment had been old Heyhouses School, there was now a choice of venue: the Parish Church rooms; Roman Catholic schools; the Baptist church school room; the Church Lads' hut; the YMCA hut; the Hotel Majestic Theatre, and many more. Under the Local Government Act of 1894, St Anne's-on-Sea and a portion of Marton became part of Lytham – an important step towards Charter Day (when Lytham amalgamated with St Annes to become Lytham St Annes) some thirty years later.

The carriage drive from Lytham to St Anne's described a hundred years ago is a reminder of what the Lytham St Anne's Nature Reserve is trying to preserve today:

> The walk was delicious. Collaterally there were billow-like heaps of sand covered with long, wavy grass and golden gorse. We got a rare exchange of wild flowers and melody for the dirge of depression and hard times we had left behind in Manchester. Climbing a starr hill of the first magnitude, a fine view was to be had in the clear air of Blackpool, Lytham, Preston, the whole of the Fylde and the hills of Bleasdale.

Once again sightings of kestrels, stonechats, skylarks, cuckoos, sedge warblers, linnets, wrens and a rich variety of moths and butterflies have been made amid litter-free areas of evening primroses. Many of the plant species listed by Hugh Holmes in 1810 are still to be found.

Confucius is often quoted as saying that to understand the present we must study the past. The sterling work of the Lytham Heritage Group in collecting old photographs, artefacts and documents is making that possible. It is hoped that the following photographs, coupled with the memories of people who have known Lytham St Anne's over the years, will make our walking in the footsteps of past generations even more pleasant.

Catherine Rothwell

One

Lytham

A two-horse landau with a top-hatted coachman waiting in Park Street, Lytham, 1900s.

The eighteenth-century brass chandelier and family monuments in St Michael's church, Kirkham, show that the Cliftons of Westby, Clifton and Kirkham were associated with Lytham for many centuries, Sir William living in the time of William Rufus (William II). It was Thomas Clifton, born in 1728, who decided to rebuild Lytham Hall and to reside there: the strong family connection is shown in the Clifton papers. A stone from the old tower bears the arms of Clifton, and a stone coffin and the sixteenth-century bowl of a font had been preserved, but in the early months of 1993 these were stolen. (Courtesy of the *Lancashire Evening Post*)

This water-colour sketch of Lytham Hall around 1600, occasionally displayed by the Lancashire Record Office, is the earliest reference to the hall and its surroundings. Through the ages various spellings of the settlement have been used, including Leddun, Lidum, Lethum, Lichun, Lythum and Lythcombe, and in later years the familiar Lytham. (Courtesy of J.T. Hilton Esq., Lord of the Manor of Lytham)

This 'Glimpse of Old Lytham' issued with 'Scrutator's' notes shows Clifton Street before the days of motorized traffic. A special Whit Week event was the annual race meeting held on The Green between Mr Cookson's New Mill, built in 1805, and Saltcotes. All of the local farmers entered their best horses for the races.

In 1830s Lytham, shown in P.H. Whittle's *Marina*, were Edmondson and Burnet, coal merchants, John Edmondson, grocer, Margaret and Mary Banister, milliners, Thomas Bonney, blacksmith, and his son Thomas, a butcher, while Alice Critchley was a grocer and confectioner. The number of lodging houses reflects Lytham's rise as a sea-bathing area, Nathan Leigh, Ann Mercer, Sarah Taylor and Jonathan Salthouse being examples of keepers. Ann Lillyman ran the Clifton Arms Inn with its cold and warm baths, and James Coup offered the same facilities. Fine houses on the beach were let furnished to families at 1 1⁄2 to 3 guineas per week, and lodgings away from the sea could be obtained for 4s. 6d. A cottage was let for 10s. 6d. per week per bed in season, but out of season was available for less.

The Wallis engraving of W.H. Bartlett's drawing of Lytham in 1840 shows, almost opposite the Clifton Hotel, what was known as Charlie's Mast. Erected by Charlie Townsend, the original was made from a cart shaft. Charlie was a mine of information on shipping and the mast became such a landmark that the Improvement Commissioners agreed to its maintenance. In its early years a lantern was placed on the mast as a guide to mariners entering the River Ribble at night, and at its foot was a wooden figurehead taken from a wrecked sailing ship. The sentinel windmill in those days had canvas sails. Much shipping is in evidence, as are the fine buildings flanking The Green, including (on the right) St Peter's Roman Catholic church, built in 1839. Behind the mill is the old lifeboat house, put up by John Talbot Clifton on the site of a brick kiln.

Queen of the Ocean, because of her sleek lines and spread of canvas, recalls to the minds of locals two well-known ships from windjammer days: *Hoghton Tower* of the White Star Line, under Captain D. Murray, made her first 73-day voyage from Liverpool on 26 June 1869 with seventy passengers; *Dallam Tower* was the best-known ship owned by Greenshield Cowie & Co. of Lancaster. Several Lytham sea captains sailed round the world.

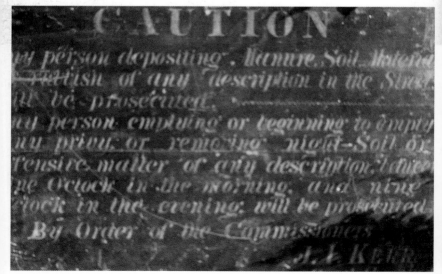

The Customs Watch House was built around 1844. After a furious storm on Christmas Day 1852 which destroyed the newly built wall along the seafront, the schooner, Pheasant of Preston, which was laden with coal, was flung hard against the Watch House. One of the boats used by the customs men ended up near the railway, and the fishing fleet was washed away together with many pleasure boats. No longer in existence, the Watch House possibly originated as a lookout. Lytham, established as a port before Preston, had four customs men ready to apprehend smugglers. Contraband was put into cellars which were also used as a mortuary for drowned bodies. Thomas Cookson met ships anchored in the Ribble to collect the squire's dues. Every Bonfire Night there was a great burning of driftwood and wreckage near the site of Lytham Pier.

Opposite below: This 'Caution: Night Soil' notice, Lytham, dated 12 May 1858, when J.I. Kerr was local surveyor, warns: 'Any person depositing manure, night soil ... rubbish of any description in the streets will be prosecuted.' In 1890 Lytham's night soil was dumped in a hollow on The Green opposite the present location of Grosvenor Street.

This stone cross, of which only the base is original, is reputedly on the spot where St Cuthbert's body rested for a while on its long journey back to Durham. An early Record Office document (the Foundation Charter of Lytham Cell) reveals some interesting details: 'All my estate of Lytham was given by Richard Fitz Roger in Edward III's reign to St Cuthbert and the monks of Durham ... From the ditch on the western side of Kilgrimol [known later as Lytham Common] over which I have erected a cross and from the same ditch and cross eastward beyond the Great Moss and Balholme [Balham] the brook runs towards Shincbriggs [Sluice Bridge].' This document defines the 'bounds' of the monks' land, and the cross referred to marks the boundary at the hamlet of Cross Slack.

St Cuthbert's church. Ancient documents (see opposite) refer to 'gifts of minstralles and other beggars and the payment of Peter's Pence'. A 'walking brief' for the repair of St Cuthbert's church was granted by the King in 1764, allowing the churchwardens to make a house-to-house collection. 'Ministers, curates, preachers and persons called Quakers are by all persuasive arguments asked to contribute.'

Cross Slack was once called Church Yard Slack as it was originally the site of a religious oratory. In Saxon times fishermen's huts existed here but all were gradually washed into the sea. A small public house kept by Mr Harrison on ground rising above Cross Slack and known as Stony Hill remained until the early 1800s.

Lytham Institute in Clifton Street, built in 1878 for £3,000, is now Lytham Library. In the early 1900s a Literary Society gave Shakespearean readings, while lectures were arranged and learned papers read by university professors from Manchester and Liverpool. In 1900 the institute had a fine reading room containing three thousand books, two billiard rooms with four tables, and a lecture hall. One room is now reserved for the work of the Lytham Heritage Group.

John Butcher of Butcher's Cottages (homes were then known merely by the surname of the occupant) was a well-known Lytham poacher in the mid-1800s. When the building of St Anne's started in about 1875, the good shooting was spoiled somewhat and the squire's guests complained.

Leach Lodge Farm, with one of the Jameson family dispensing corn for the poultry from an antique 'piggin' container. The barn at Leach Lodge was a favourite for dances, accompanied by the fiddler Will Wade from Mad Nook. The late Kathleen Eyre, historian, recorded that farmer John Jameson was as light as a feather on his feet.

The Market House was built for £1,000 in 1848 and provided room for twenty-three stalls. In 1868 Lady Eleanor Cecily Clifton paid for the clock to be added. Beneath it was a room where the Improvement Commissioners held meetings. The trees, planted in 1850, were all supplied by the Clifton family.

Lytham Volunteer Band of the 2nd East Lancashire Regiment outside the entrance to Lytham Hall in 1897. The Lytham Subscription Band used the old Lytham Gasworks for practice rooms. The British Legion Club Band had the misfortune to lose instruments, music and uniforms in a fire, but it managed to set itself up again.

A pony and trap were used by Mr Clifton's agent to travel between farms and cottages. This scene from the 1880s is thought to be outside Headroomgate Farm. In 1606 when Cuthbert Clifton purchased the Manor of Lytham from Sir Richard Molyneux the price was £4,300.

The crowning of the Rose Queen on Lytham Club Day almost a hundred years ago. The upper room of J. Sefton's shop is crowded with spectators. There are shiny top hats, bowlers, homburgs and toques. The Boys' Brigade is in full force and a charming group of white-clad, befrilled small girls takes centre stage. The seated, bearded patriarchal figure on the dais is Crimean War veteran A. Wykeham Clifton. Club Day processions in early years followed a route via Hastings Road, Westby Street, Station Road, Clifton Street, Church Road, Lowther Terrace, the beach, the Cottage Hospital and back to Market Square by 1 p.m. Led by five rose-laden bicycles, the Band of Hope, Rechabites and Temperance Society, Oddfellows and Mechanics followed. The Lytham Volunteer Band, and Preston Temperance and Subscription Bands provided the music. Among the many floats was 'Ally Sloper', drawn by a donkey. There was a song about this music-hall entertainer at the time.

Cockling on the Horsebank, 1877. The Horsebank is known to have been green pasture for cattle in 1590. Kilgrimol cemetery was attached to Lytham priory in 1400, and winds whistling eerily among the starr hills led to stories of phantom voices and muffled church bells from the buried cemetery, obliterated by blown sand and the encroachment of the banks of the River Ribble.

The lifeboat *Laura Janet*, donated by James Chadwick of Preston, was present at the opening of St Anne's Pier on 15 June 1885. Lifeboatmen turned out from Lytham, St Anne's and Blackpool, with three thousand visitors unaware of the *Mexico* disaster that lay one year ahead. At the end of the pier is SS *Wellington*.

The gentleman in the light-coloured garment in the centre of this photograph of 1893 is John Cooling, captain of the Shaw Cycling Club. At least three penny-farthings can be seen. The flat countryside beside the sea was loved by cycling clubs, as indicated by the many Cyclists' Rest inns that existed then.

A view of 'An Old Thatch Cottage, Marton', available as a popular postcard. This is Wade's Cottage at the junction of Cherry Tree Road and Clifton Road. The Clifton Road sign can be seen on the side partly hidden by rambler roses. This site was developed by a builder who swept away this picturesque homestead and erected flats.

No. 16 is an example of one of the larger gas-operated tramcars that ran in the days of the Blackpool, St Anne's & Lytham Tramways Co. The *Tramway Review* produced a complete history of the tramways of Lytham St Anne's some fifty years ago.

A Dicconson Terrace doorway with its 1825 fanlight. The terrace derives its name from the marriage, in 1819, of Edward Clifton to Elizabeth, co-heir of Thomas Swarbrick of Ecclestone and Wrightington, whose children were allowed by Royal Charter to assume the name and arms of Dicconson.

Lytham Hall. In the early 1600s Sir Cuthbert Clifton, the first Squire of Lytham, built a house on the site of the Benedictine priory which had been founded in 1190 and dissolved by Henry VIII's commissioners. As a recusant frowned upon for his Roman Catholic religion, he had given his hall at Westby, Kirkham, for the use of the Catholics of Lytham. Registered in the records of Kirkham is the payment of 'Sunday shillings' by recusants. On moving to Lytham he built a chapel, and when Thomas Clifton rebuilt Lytham Hall between 1757 and 1764 he incorporated this chapel, which was used for Mass until 1800 when the tithe barn was pressed into service and the officiating priest given the house called Woodlands. Thomas Clifton employed the famous architect John Carr of York on the rebuilding, although the servants' hall, kitchens and outbuildings retained the vestiges of the original priory structure.

An early steam trawler set with canvas sails. Lytham had the first fishing company on the Fylde coast. Before the lifeboat was provided, fishermen rescued shipwrecked mariners, and Wheeler's *Manchester Chronicle* records on 27 December 1817 how a Lytham fishing boat picked up twelve survivors from the Corry, a Newry packet boat, though two people later died of exposure.

Puffin, one of the Lytham Shipbuilding & Engineering Co.'s vessels, like the cargo steamer *Cecil*, was very strong and fitted with a hauling windlass. The SS *Luna* was built following an order from Cape Town, while twin-screw tug *Rodas* was specially designed for heavy towing at sea.

Bath Street, Lytham, was set with cobblestones in the 1840s and had mosaic patterns in front of each door. By 1984 damage caused by parked cars was alarming residents, and, under a joint Lancashire County Council and Fylde Borough Council plan, twenty Victorian-style cast-iron bollards were erected to line the street. (Courtesy of the *Lancashire Evening Post*)

The Market Hall, with the Estate Office on the right. On the 1894 Club Day, itinerant vendors took up position here and remained until midnight. The Lytham Minstrels, appearing at the pier, joined them and by 11 p.m. Market Square was impassable. Lythamers were up at 5.40 the next morning when five hundred tradespeople left by train for a special trip to the Dukeries.

Unveiling the Lifeboat Monument on 23 May 1888. The worst-ever British lifeboat disaster occurred on 9 December 1886. The lifeboat crews of Southport, Lytham and St Anne's responded to distress signals from the *Mexico* of Hamburg. Of the three lifeboats only that of Lytham returned safely with *Mexico's* crew; those of Southport and St Anne's had capsized. All of St Anne's crew perished and thirteen of the fifteen-strong Southport crew drowned also. The Humane Society of France presented a Diploma of Honour to the town. In the crowd are Robert Hargreaves (Chairman of the Local Board), Thomas Bradley (Clerk) and John Talbot Clifton.

The Green Drive in this postcard of 1907 reflects the great tree-planting programme that the Cliftons started in 1850, an expensive project which some think may have driven them abroad. In the 1900s the *Lytham St Anne's Press*, edited by Robert Clarke, referred to 'the noble, green Cathedral of the Green Drive', a favourite bridle path and walking area. The whole park attached to Lytham Hall expressed the ideals of eighteenth-century landscape gardening.

Lytham Green, c. 1903, appears little changed today. The pathway where the lady walks with her children is opposite Bannister Street. It was in the mid-nineteenth century that the Commissioners commenced levelling the ground and laying the turf.

Tony Croft's newsagents, Warton Street, 1903, features glass and wrought iron in its veranda. An agent for Cadbury's chocolate and the Cash bakery, Tony also sold Capstan cigarettes and pipe tobacco. A placard in the foreground advertises the *Guardian*. Miss Lillian Machel's grandparents owned the shop at this time.

Annie Johnson, the first Rose Queen of Lytham in 1894, was reported as looking 'extremely beautiful in a white dress. She wore a wreath of exquisite roses.' She was crowned in Market Square by Mr A. Wykeham Clifton, and afterwards had a meal at the Baths Assembly Hall. The procession included floats, bands, troupes of donkeys, shrimping girls and minstrels. Sports were organized in the afternoon and a funfair powered by a steam organ in the Square was held at night by gaslight.

Crowning of a Rose Queen on Club Day, c. 1928. 'Lytham Picture Palace nightly at 8' is advertised on the side of the Lytham Baths. The white-bearded figure is A. Wykeham Clifton, a member of the Clifton family who frequently crowned rose queens. Squire J. Talbot Clifton is seated on the right.

Market Square, Lytham, c. 1900, with a band playing before spectators. The large monument in the foreground was later moved. Long ago the Market Square had a market cross and fish stones. The Market Hotel, later called the County and Commercial, was built in 1808, at which time Henry Street was known as Duck Lane.

Clifton-owned farm in the Lytham area, 1900. The farm appears to be given over to milk production and growing vegetables. Almost every inn and cottage at this time kept a pig. Strictures were laid down regarding methods of farming, with rents being payable on quarter days.

Ballam Road, c. 1906. Handmade bricks of local clay were shaped and baked at Ballam (also known as Balham and Balholme) near Eastham Hall. In 1837 there was also a brick-making works near Ribchester Road where the clay was excavated. Most Lytham houses of that date, with their warm red appearance, were made from local bricks.

Before and during the sixteenth century, cottages were made from those materials available, such as peat, clay and heather or cobblestones. The cruck (cross) form on the gable ends was achieved by crossing two tree trunks and connecting them with a ridge pole. The sides comprised branches plastered with clay and the roof was thatched. This cottage is at Treates near Lytham. The little girl became Mrs Gibson, now aged over eighty.

Saltcote Cottages were used by saltwellers (salt manufacturers) over two hundred years ago. Two-wheeled carts ('sand coupes') collected salty sand which had to be kept dry. Straw or peat acted as a filter and the sand, once used, piled up into a 'saltcote hill'. The brine was boiled for about four hours to drive off the liquid.

Goodson's Special Show. Fashionable ladies in Lytham and St Anne's, besides patronizing Goulden's in Blackpool, took the train to Goodson's of Manchester for a high-fashion garment like this one of 1902. Was it an ancestor of mine who was reported in the local newspaper? 'Mrs Rothwell looked well in grenat cashmere with velvet zonave edged with crystal passementerie and a grenat white hat.' Black sequins, jet, silk accordian pleating, petunia silk, black velvet ribbon, lace and deep cream Tuscan straw were all used to wonderful effect.

Dr Poole, a Lytham resident, 9 October 1911. This learned bachelor, who for a time was tutor to de Vere Clifton at Lytham Hall, wrote poems and at the request of the Urban District Council prepared a booklet on Lytham in the Corporation Guide series, which was illustrated with photographs by Hedges and Son. Dr Poole made a special study of the document relating to the Cell of Lytham (see pp. 16 and 17) and the 'walking brief' connected with the repair of St Cuthbert's church in 1764.

Lytham West Beach. Some fashionable houses on East and West Beach were furnished by Pitts of London Road, Manchester, whose *New Illustrated Furnishing Guide* contained eight hundred designs, with prices from 15$\frac{1}{2}$ to 2,000 guineas. In 1905 Pitts boasted that its furniture was considered by experts to be worth double the prices they asked.

Wrought-iron gates designed by Christopher Wren for Lytham Hall and given as a wedding present to an earlier squire, February 1966. They were placed under a preservation order when the fate of the hall was uncertain. A conference centre, museum and art gallery were all suggestions put forward as to its future use. The hall was finally purchased by Guardian Royal Exchange Assurance. (Courtesy of the *Lancashire Evening Post*)

Lytham Common, painted by Richard Ansdell, RA, appeared as an engraving in *The Illustrated London News* of 25 February 1854. On the right, alongside the driftwood, the artist has captured the beautiful yellow evening primrose, a plant that grew in great profusion at Lytham St Anne's until much disturbed by the removal of the sand hills. (Courtesy of the *Evening Gazette*)

Swiss Cottage Lodge, Lytham Hall Park. Although great tracts of land were available in the early nineteenth century, the terms for building leases remained feudal-based. Even when they were extended from forty to sixty years, few people cared to build because they were restrained from selling or even letting their houses without the consent of the Cliftons.

This perimeter wall (running behind the mansions built on Clifton Drive) of pebbled panels within brick, capped with coping stones, is an example of fine building work. In other sections a piece of lead has been inserted where the coping stones meet which has preserved the wall down the years and through all weathers. West of the White Church, Fairhaven, doorways have cappings of the same stone.

The White Cottage on West Beach supposedly occupies the site of the hunting lodge used by the squire's visitors. Yates's map of 1786 features a small building which stood there until 1812, occupied by William Rawstorne, an attorney. By 1840 the building had been extended but in 1934 the wine cellar was filled in.

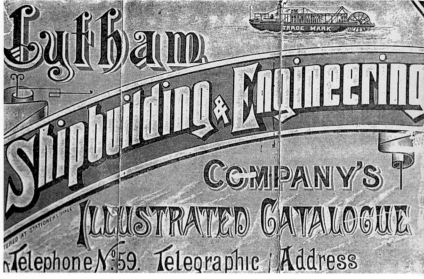

Lytham Shipbuilding & Engineering Co. catalogue. By 1908 Lytham Shipyard had become a large concern, with two to three hundred men building vessels. The last to be built in the boatyard was the *Drake*, launched in 1954. Among nine hundred listed ships coming from Lytham Shipyard were *Larchfield*, *Naracuta*, *Perseverance*, *Ribble Queen*, *Rowanfield*, *Ashfield*, *Eugenia* and *Fenella*.

The Ship Inn and Royal Hotel, one of Lytham's historic buildings. In 1820 its charges were 3s. 6d. per day. Stagecoaches ran daily during the season and there was a 'New Theatre' where travelling companies performed. By 1828 the Wheat Sheaf Inn and a row of ancient thatched cottages were demolished, The Green was levelled and the building of the Promenade was begun.

'Lytham with its sylvan beauty and quiet tranquil air of contentment' was how the resort was described in 1902. Then the sea lapped the beach, and this old photograph taken that year proves that paddling was possible.

Park Road from Market Square, 1890, showing Crozier's confectionery and refreshment rooms. Mr Crozier was an agent for Schweppes Table Waters. What may be a knife grinder's machine is parked by the lamp and a few doors away is Cookson's circulating library.

A wreck on the Horsebank, 1870. Before a lifeboat was available, onlookers could only stand helpless. In February 1839 a Spanish schooner, *Felix Destino*, met its doom despite a brave rescue attempt. Hugh Holmes refers to 'the famous Horsebank where many a mariner has been swallowed up by the waves and where much treasure lies buried'.

The *Charles Biggs* lifeboat, with crew and local dignitaries alongside, on a Lifeboat Saturday in Clifton Square, 1891. Tom Clarkson (standing in the lifeboat, far right) was in charge when the crew of the *Mexico* was rescued. Mrs Fletcher's confectionery and bread bakery in the background was later replaced by De Grey's Buildings.

The Promenade, 1908. With its pier, green, windmill, clean air and orderliness, Lytham was a splendid place for rest and recuperation. This card, issued by E. & E. Torry of Lytham, was written from the Cottage Hospital by a patient about to return home.

This photograph, c. 1890, lent by a life-long resident, reminds us that Lytham was once famous for its potted shrimps. They are mentioned in verse by Judge Parry of the local circuit who wrote delightful stories for children. The shrimpers went barefoot across the sands with large nets and baskets. Club Day 1887 featured 'Shrimp girls in lorry' as item 16 in the procession.

Lytham College, 1904. A boys' boarding school, this building stands in Clifton Drive near the corner of Woodlands Road, Ansdell. To the left the school had a tennis court. The property has been converted into flats but one of the entrances bears a reminder of its history, being clearly marked 'Boys'.

Cross Slack Farm, near St Anne's Old Links, has been the home of the Gillett family since the 1800s, successive generations eking out their farming by musseling and shrimping. George, born in 1851, was one of a party who saw the first stone lighthouse fall, its foundations undermined by the waves. The time was 12.15 p.m. on Thursday 22 January 1863.

The wreck of the steamship *Huntcliff* in 1894 was an exciting event and its repercussions continued for weeks. *Huntcliff* had set out from Liverpool at 2 p.m. one Sunday in February carrying only ballast, so a tremendous amount of its hull was exposed to the wind and waves. Such was the wind force and flood of seas inland that day, rabbits and hares were seen running down the streets of Lytham. 'If we had only had half a cargo we would have been able to steam against it', said Captain Howell. The crew of twenty-seven men included five Arabs and a Zulu who looked after the stoking and, unknown to anyone, there were also two stowaways who hoped to get off at Cardiff. In the teeth of the gale *Huntcliff* rolled helplessly, until it bumped, undamaged, near the convalescent home, some 50 yds from the sand hills. News of the stranding of such a magnificent ship brought in the crowds until the scene resembled a fairground, with photographers, ice-cream vendors, fruit sellers and eight hundred spectators. How to move the *Huntcliff* was a problem, but as she was insured for £35,000 the underwriters were determined to refloat her. On 24 February the task was complete, to the relief of the St Anne's people as some of the crew had got drunk and the Arabs had been embroiled in a knife fight.

Shannon, built at Belfast in 1887, was one of many ships seen from Lytham in 1900. Dr Poole described the scene as 'an ever moving panorama of ships, steamers, and small craft. Across the estuary is Southport glistening like a jewel, to the left broad meadows, wooded hills and hollows with their white homesteads.' *Adriatic*, built at Belfast in 1872, is shown below.

Fylde's first named lifeboat, in 1851, was the *Eleanor Cecily*. Lytham lifeboatmen saved four crewmen from a schooner in 1857, five in 1878 and twenty-three from the barque *Mermaid* in 1883. The steam tug, *Secret*, was lost with its eight-man crew in 1892. Three years later, in the greatest frost for sixty years, the sea froze over.

Childrens Corner, Ansdell

Mr A.A. Watts, chemist, issued this photograph of the Children's Corner at Ansdell on a sunny summer day in the early 1900s. There were also postcards of a Children's Corner in Lytham.

A single-horse family omnibus used by the London and North Western Railway, formerly the Preston & Wyre, was the usual conveyance from the station to lodgings or hotels on the Promenade. On the roof were strapped bicycles and luggage, while the family travelled inside.

A walk on the pier at Lytham in 1928 revealed its fancy wrought-ironwork, lamps, ornamental shelters and seating. This now-vanished pier, built in 1864, was damaged in October 1903. In the year this postcard was written the Pavilion was destroyed by fire.

Lytham soldiers on their way to the South African War. Seven Lytham men volunteered for service, and with others from Fylde were stationed at Fleetwood Barracks. They had a great send-off, with dinner at the County Hotel and many gifts: 5s. each, two pairs of socks, cake, a Bible, gloves, mufflers, capes, shirts and stationery. Conveyed to the station in a procession of landaus, accompanied by police, councillors and lifeboatmen, they were carried shoulder-high onto the platform with much cheering and flag waving to the tune of 'The Soldiers of the Queen'. These seven were privates E. Barton, O. Cartmell, W.E. Matthews, Thomas Webster, C. Whitehead, F. Wilson and W. Fisher. Six months later they returned to the same tumultuous welcome. It is thought this photograph was taken by Mr Hedges, in later years a 'Royal Photographer'.

Mr C.W. Johnson, a cornet player, was Club Day bandmaster for forty years. He walked with the band on Kirkham and Lytham Club Days and Rose Queen Festivals, and on Armistice Remembrance Days played the Last Post at the Cenotaph. Once a marine engineer at Cammell Laird's Shipyard, he also worked in Lytham Shipyard, serving his apprenticeship prior to 1914. Here he is seen in uniform during the First World War.

Lytham Amateur Orchestra, portrayed on a poster of 1900. It played at bazaars, fêtes and musical soirées under the direction of Mr W.F. Holden, giving selections from light operas such as *The Mikado* and *The Gondoliers*.

H. Thornley, high-class grocer of Lytham Road, his shop windows packed with hams and bacon, was one of many busy Lytham premises. Shops in Lytham St Anne's in the 1900s included The Bee Hive, 20 St Anne's Road West, 'sole agents for Aston flannels and Storm serges'; Chadwick's cash drapers, 37 Clifton Street, 'muslin 3d. half a yard'; and W.E. Garlick, butcher, 46 Clifton Street.

Lytham tram No. 1 advertises Brand's Essence, a famous invalid food at the beginning of the twentieth century. A leisurely group of bystanders and the tram driver watch the photographer, who has nicely positioned the delivery boys with their bicycles. The swan-necked lamp and early automobile are typical of the time.

A group of nurses and patients assemble outside Lytham Cottage Hospital, 1890s. The small hospital, opened in 1871 as a result of fever epidemic the previous year, was provided by Colonel John Talbot Clifton and for many years also took patients from St Anne's.

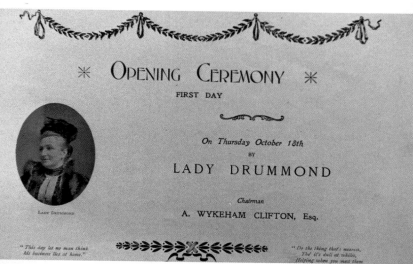

※ OPENING CEREMONY ※

FIRST DAY

On Thursday October 18th

BY

LADY DRUMMOND

Chairman

A. WYKEHAM CLIFTON, Esq.

LADY DRUMMOND

" This day let no man think
his business lies at home."

" Do the thing that's nearest,
Tho' it's dull at whiles,
Helping when you meet them

Front page of Grand Bazaar brochure. Lytham Cottage Hospital held a three-day Grand Bazaar in the Baths Assembly Rooms in October 1900. A stall selling mauve and white dresses was run by three ladies, helped by Nellie Oram. They advertised in verse:
Come to the sale. Come to the sale.
Come by trams and come by the Rail.

Lytham's first recruits, enlisted by Sergeant Howard for Lord Kitchener's army. The First Volunteer Company was formed on 13 December 1849 at a meeting held at Edmondson's shop in Market Square. Among the sixty-nine volunteers were familiar Lytham names including Fisher, Cookson, Hincksman, Swann, Whiteside and Salthouse.

The Cottage Hospital, Lytham, with landaus outside when the three-day Grand Bazaar was held to raise funds, 1900. Leonard Pilkington set up a shooting gallery as one of the attractions and a 'leading occultist' read palms.

A Rotary photograph of West Beach, Lytham, 1906, gives a good view of the children's swingboats, with the ice-cream booth behind. Around this time, 'Blind Martin', always accompanied by his faithful dog, trundled a harmonium on wheels through Lytham's streets collecting pennies.

The opening of Ansdell Institute, 1909. This was a prestigious event and residents donned Sunday clothes. It would appear that at this time everyone wore a hat and the remark, 'You are not dressed without one', firmly applied. The building has served the community well as meeting place, dance hall, billiard room and club. Until recently there was a bowling green adjacent.

A tram in Market Square at Lytham, c. 1905, seems greatly overloaded with both passengers and advertisements. T. Sharp of The Crescent offers accommodation for sixty at his tearooms. Epp's Cocoa, Durant's Herbal Pills and Pritchard's Teething Powders were all familiar remedies at that time, and all were emblazoned on tramcars.

Lytham Windmill and Lifeboat House, early 1900s. The fire that raged in the mill one night in 1918 consumed all of the woodwork, including the autographed panel bearing the signatures of Sir Harry Lauder and Sir Martin Harvey. It was caused when the wind suddenly changed direction and sent the sails into reverse, literally sparking off the conflagration.

First World War soldiers marching to Squire's Gate after drilling. Among the officers serving in the Lytham Volunteer Rifle Corps were Major Hincksman, Captain James Fair, Captain Talbot Fair, Lieutenant Outram and Lieutenant Lomax. Familiar Lytham names among the drill instructors were Moore, Clarkson, Collinson and Hardman.

The Lytham Pier disaster occurred on 6 October 1903, when two sand barges drifting before the gale dragged anchor and sliced the pier in two. Fortunately the Pavilion escaped damage.

The parish church of St John the Divine, built on the seafront at Lytham in 1849, is surmounted by a spire 140 ft high. Until 1875 the steeple contained one bell, but in that year six tenor bells were installed by Mears and Staibank. A strong band of ringers between 1911 and 1913 pealed out 'Violet', 'Merchants Return', 'Duke of York', etc., but because of the corrosion by sea air of the ironwork in the belfry, the bells became loose and ringing was curtailed. The Revd John Carlisle, himself a ringer, successfully conducted a peal of 'Bob Minor' in 1983 and since then a dedicated team has worked on the bells' restoration. The bells of St John were rededicated on 10 January 1993.

The first intake of seventy-four boys assembled outside King Edward VII Grammar School, September 1908. The Trustees of the Annual Lytham Charities passed a resolution on 8 December 1901, 'That it is desirable to erect within the ancient parish of Lytham a good Secondary School for boys in which special attention is given to modern languages, mathematics and science.' A site in the sand hills was selected and architectural plans approved. The school opened in 1908 under Headmaster H. Bompass Smith and four assistant masters. The first magazine, the *Kestrel*, appeared in 1911. Hardy Parsons, an old boy of the school who died during the First World War, was awarded the Victoria Cross.

King Edward School rugby football team, 1909. Building was still in progress when the first term commenced. Near the school was the Lytham Old Rifle Corps shooting range and target.

Young footballers at Park View Road, Lytham, 1910. The Cliftons ensured an open view from the hall to the sea by the formation of Lowther Gardens and the large cricket field near Seafield House.

The Rose Queen's landau, escorted by boy scouts and lavishly decorated with paper roses, photographed by Mr J. Wolstenholme on Club Day, c. 1926. One scout seems to be envying the pageboy riding in luxury.

St John's Sunday School, Lytham Club Day, 1903. This lavishly decorated tableau features the 'Grecian Girls', with the banner of St John's Sunday School behind them. Horses released from mundane work on these occasions were well groomed, their brasses shining like gold.

Two

St Anne's-on-Sea

Leafy Wood Street, St Anne's, 1902.

The late Mr. W. J. Porritt,
One of the makers of St. Annes.

The late Mr. Thomas Fair,
Who, as Agent to the Clifton Estates,
promoted the town of St. Annes.

The late Mr. Elijah Hargreaves,
Founder of the St. Annes Land Company.

W.J. Porritt, Thomas Fair and Elijah Hargreaves are remembered in Lytham St Anne's as great pioneers, and they featured in the souvenir brochure when Lytham and St Anne's united in 1922. Mr W.J. Porritt was a builder of quality houses, Thomas Fair was agent to the Clifton Estates and Elijah Hargreaves was founder of the St Anne's Land and Building Company, consisting of Rossendale businessmen. In 1874 this trio was alerted to the fact that the railway was extended from Lytham to Blackpool. They approached the Clifton Estate with a view to leasing the site of St Anne's for a term of 1,100 years. The foundation stone of the new town was laid in March 1875 by the six-year-old J. Talbot Clifton, Squire of Lytham.

A very early photograph of North Promenade, St Anne's, with what appears to be the lighthouse in the centre. Many visitors walked out to the lighthouse and left their names or initials carved on its structure. An Act to confer further powers on the UDC of St Anne's was passed on 14 August 1896, in order that it might make further improvements as the town grew in popularity.

Cottages around Commonside. Lytham Hall and the vicarage were the only buildings of any size in Lytham in 1720, when forty small dwellings and barns suffered from high tides sweeping inland. Richard Bawbell and ten others requested charity of £2,055 but received only £103, three guineas coming from Mr William Elston of Commonside.

St Anne's church, Heyhouses, which seated four hundred people, marked the establishment of St Anne's as a real town. Lady Eleanor Cecily Clifton sponsored the building and gave a peal of eight bells in 1890 in memory of the Clifton family. Three fishermen brothers, John, Joseph and William Melling, who lived in three cottages in Mellings Lane, helped to cart the bricks.

St Anne's Square in the 1890s, then known as Hydro Terrace, looking towards the sea. Hargreaves' pharmacy and Garnett's tailors are in the vicinity of the present-day Edinburgh Woollen Mill.

Almost a hundred years ago this photograph and description of the South Promenade at St Anne's-on-Sea were published in *Round the Coast: Photographs of the Chief Seaside Places in Great Britain*. 'Amidst wild sandhills a beautiful town has taken the place of what was a bleak, barren waste ... a thoroughly well-planned town of between 3–4,000 people. There are a great number of trim villas standing in well-kept grounds. St. Anne's is essentially a resort for families; children desire no more enjoyable pastime than a ramble among the sandhills on each side of the town.' It is interesting to see a line of donkeys and the recently erected Lifeboat Monument in splendid isolation.

The Abraham Ormerod Convalescent Home, built in 1890 and opened by Colonel Clifton's widow, Lady Eleanor Cecily, did great work in helping handicapped children. It is seen here before the chapel was built. Among the early buildings that rose from the sand hills were the pebble-built Starr Hills—occupied by Richard Ansdell and later by Major Hincksman—The Willows, The Elms and Edenfield.

Siah Cartmell, the last lighthouse keeper, stands outside St Anne's wooden lighthouse, set on sand dunes to replace a stone-built structure which collapsed in 1863, having been undermined by the sea. No longer needed after 1901, the wooden building was pulled down.

Pine Cottage, the first rated house in St Anne's, was the home of William Heap. Mr Heap's father arrived in 1874 with three other builders, Messrs Shepherd, Walmsley and Smith. 'For shopping it was rather a long way to go—either Lytham or Blackpool', William recalled. 'We went to Lytham Congregational Church by walking along the railway lines and to the old Heyhouses School at the top of St Anne's Road East over the "cops". After 18 months at Pine Cottage we went to live on Church Road and houses were being rushed up in all directions. At the grocer's shop coal was sold. Weighing was so exact, the shopkeeper's wife would cut a Pontefract Cake in half.' As early as 1819 one house had appeared among the sandy wastes. This was built by Thomas Moore who later erected a row of cottages fronting the sea. His son, Dr Alexander Moore of Preston, followed suit. Layton Hawes church, another early building where the Revd Greene became the first curate, was partly the gift of Peter Hesketh Fleetwood who owned all the land.

During Sunday church parades Lytham Green and St Anne's Promenade (shown here) were ablaze with fashionably dressed ladies with their escorts and well-mannered children accompanied by nursemaids. The sunsets were remarked upon by Richard Ansdell, RA, who settled here and gave his name to that part which adjoins Lytham.

St Anne's Square property erected by Robert Wade, shown in an *Evening Gazette* photograph of the early 1900s. To the right Gill and Read are doing good business in camp stools and folding chairs. The Lancashire and Yorkshire Bank was situated here, as were the Council Chamber and Urban District Council offices.

Lamp and fountain, St Anne's Promenade, 1889. The spacious, well-planned quality of the town was apparent from an early date, as shown here. A much later photograph proves that the charming drinking fountain has weathered the storms to this day, no doubt helped by its 'cast iron constitution'. Healthy Fylde air often resulted in long life for dwellers by the sea. One Lytham St Anne's lady, Mrs Barton, whose maiden name was Harrison, was born on 18 January 1785. She had nineteen grandchildren and thirty-two great-grandchildren. Her husband, a farmer, died in 1842, but the fourth generation remained in South Fylde, one of her sons being seventy-five years of age. She could recall the battles of the Nile and Waterloo, Georges III's Jubilee, the accession of Queen Victoria, the coming of the railways, the repeal of the Corn Laws and the days when meal was £6 per load. When interviewed by a reporter in 1887, she said she had never had a serious illness. (Courtesy of the *Evening Gazette*)

Tom Clarkson, coxswain, was in charge when the Lytham lifeboat rescued the crew of the iron barque, *Mexico*, which had anchored on the Horsebank. The Southport lifeboat *Eliza Fernley* was lost, with all but two of her crew drowned. Thirteen men, the entire crew of the *Laura Janet* of St Anne's, also lost their lives. (See p. 28.)

When Louise Stubbs became Mrs Gillett she retired from child minding to bring up a family of her own. She is seen here as a girl of eighteen in typical Victorian attire: jet buttons, lace at throat and cuffs, cameo, draped black dress and severe hairstyle. Nicholas Gillett of Willow Cottage was an expert thatcher. To the uninitiated it is amazing how much reed or straw is necessary for one job. Some old photographs show supplies piled as high as the cottage.

The *Mexico*, with a crew of twelve, was journeying from Hamburg to Liverpool with general cargo when a storm of exceptional fury blew up on the night of 9 December 1886. Southport, Lytham and St Anne's lifeboats responded to the *Mexico's* distress signals, the St Anne's boat leaving at 10.30 p.m. A crowd waited on the shore all night for information. From Mr Macara's house came the terrible news that bodies of seamen had been cast up. Hours later the Lytham lifeboat was sighted and a horseman, on behalf of the agonized relatives, rode into the waves, only to return with news that just one of the three boats had survived. At the inquiry into the disaster Coxswain Clarkson reported: 'As we approached the wreck four or five times the boat was full, we broke four oars. When we got to the *Mexico* we got them all off ... We put her on the port tack and a tremendous sea smacked over us. We made straight for Lytham and got home at 3.30 a.m., wet through and half drowned.' The *Mexico* was eventually repaired but finally lost in 1888. This Lancashire lifeboat disaster eclipsed anything previously recorded in the sixty-two years of the RNLI's existence.

J. Charles Dibdin, Fellow of the Royal Geographical Society, was secretary of the RNLI in the 1880s. In August 1894, in collaboration with John Ayling, he published the *Book of the Lifeboat*, which makes particular references to the sandy shallows of the Ribble Estuary off St Anne's-on-Sea: 'Three noble crews put out upon that deadly triangle of water, sand and reef on the night of December 9th 1886.'

The opening of St Anne's Pier, 1885. Local dignitaries are gathered for the launching of the *Laura Janet*. Before a change in the course of the channel occurred at St Anne's in 1897, fishing smacks and pleasure boats anchored off the pier jetty and steamboats set off with passengers for Fleetwood, Lytham, Southport, Morecambe and Liverpool.

Grand Hotel, St. Annes-on-the-Sea

Spring Brothers, publishers and printers of St Anne's, produced this postcard of the Grand Hotel opposite the sunken gardens in the days when Miss K. Holloway was the manageress. 'Going to the concert in St. George's Gardens was not much in my line', reads the message on the reverse.

St Anne's Congregational church was built in 1896. Initially a mission in Wood Street had served the Free Churches. In the early years the Congregationalists provided periodical entertainment in their Assembly Rooms and Sunday School, helped by Mr Heap and Mr Harold Porritt. The Revd W. Somerville was then the pastor. (Courtesy of the *Lancashire Evening Post*)

This St Anne's family, photographed in 1895, ran a boarding house called Ivanhoe. Hetty, who married Fred Woodhead, took a hotel on South Promenade. The menfolk were interested in cricket, theatre, music hall and concerts, collecting a wealth of theatre programmes between them. Kathleen Hall Houghton's grandfather (centre) used to recite *The Burial of Moses* at local concerts.

Charles Macara, c. 1888. Following the general appeal for funds after the *Mexico* disaster, Mr Macara made a determined effort to arouse the sympathy of Manchester people towards the RNLI. Banks, mills, warehouses and engineering shops in Manchester and Salford all contributed, and it was in this way that Lifeboat Saturday originated. The *News of the World* stated forcibly: 'There should be a Lifeboat Saturday as well as a Hospital Saturday.' Mr Macara's aim was to increase the income to £100,000 per annum, a sum that would cover retaining fees for all lifeboatmen and compensation in case of injury or death.

The Howarth family, April 1885. The parents are R.S. Howarth, born 1841, and Harriet. The children are: Ethel Maud (3), Jessie May (4), Walter(5), Elsie Marion(6), Robert W. (7) and Margaret Whittam (8). Robert W. became one of the best scholars at the Links School. His school reports, which prove a standard of excellence, are still in existence. Walter went to South Africa and corresponded regularly, but after the First World War the family never heard from him again.

James Forrest and family first came to Lytham over Freckleton Marsh in a wagonette. This photograph of Mr Forrest in his Edwardian-style suit recalls the prices and styles of eighty years ago. In 1910 it was possible to buy 'a gent's suit made to measure' for 24s. 6d. and trousers for only 8s. 11d. Ernest G. Price, tailor, 'buys for cash from the most eminent woollen manufacturers in England, Ireland and Scotland, therefore enabling him to turn out High Class garments at astonishingly low prices'.

The Lifeboat Monument soon after erection. Only five days before the barque *Mexico* was wrecked, the St Anne's crew had saved six men from the *Yan Yean* near Salter's Bank, Mr Macara telephoning the story to the Manchester newspapers. (Courtesy of the *Evening Gazette*)

Granny's Dock was named by the Commonside fishermen who anchored when seeking a safe haven. Until 1885 the dock was used by Lytham, Heyhouses and St Anne's fishermen. Here they mended nets, and cleaned and repainted their boats. Samphire or 'sandfirth' was collected and pickled in vinegar for sale to visitors.

This view of 1908 indicates the numbers pacing the pier at the height of the season. In the crowd is 'Florrie—taken whilst watching the Cadetts'. Behind can be seen part of the Moorish Pavilion which, along with the Floral Hall, was built by popular demand after the pier was extended and widened in 1904.

This photograph of crowds watching 'Cousin Freddie's' at Carlton's Cosy Corner on 6 June 1908 is especially interesting as it captured in the background the unfinished house-building on the Promenade. Keenan, Parker and Yates, joiners, builders and plumbers, established in 1903, advertised, 'Desirable villas for sale to suit purchaser'.

The pier, bandstand, promenade and monument gave impetus to the development of St Anne's. In summer a German band played in the open air, while Mr Dallas and his troupe, and Mr Carlton and his pierrots, gave performances among the sand hills. In later years the young Gracie Fields appeared. Mr W.H. Nutter was the pier manager, followed by Mr R. Cartmell.

This photograph was specially taken by David Hedges after the *Mexico* disaster of 1886. No difficulty was found in forming an entirely new crew. The name Parkinson appeared twice in the list of those who perished in the attempt to save the German crew, and six times more in the list of successors. Lifeboatmen on the Fylde coast, as elsewhere, were famed for their 'distinguished bravery and gallant conduct' (*Punch* 1892).

J.R. Taylor (1869–1951) was the founder of St Anne's fashion store. His first premises in Century Buildings, Garden Street, opened in 1901 with a staff of two. Success led to the acquisition of shops next door and two more in 1917. A major modernization of the premises was carried out in 1924. To this day it remains a family-run business, built on the old-fashioned traditions of quality and personal service.

The original James Robert Taylor was a Rochdale shirt-maker whose 1890s shop is shown here. Sadly, 'J.R.' died in 1951, the year of the store's Golden Jubilee. By 1961, its Diamond Jubilee year, the four-storey building could boast one hundred staff handling 'everything for a woman'.

St Anne's Road West, early 1900s. In the 1880s there were two wildernesses, stretching to Ansdell on the one side and Squire's Gate on the other. St Anne's Road was then known as Middle Lane.

Bathing machines at St Anne's in 1891 bearing typical advertisements for Pears soap. Perhaps it was opportune to have a cake of soap when taking the plunge. Hugh Holmes, a barber-surgeon of Lytham, wrote in the eighteenth century that, 'The natives did not bathe at all.'

A scene from the Lifeboat House, 1900. 'It was very strange,' wrote Wilson Heap, 'but we were not long in making ourselves at home with the rabbits and other game. We were eight in all with father and mother.' No doubt Mrs Leadbetter's potted shrimps in small white pots were teatime favourites for visitors, and for the Heap family too.

St Anne's-on-Sea from the pier, with the Southdown Hotel (on the right), later called the Hydro, run by Miss Spyree who described it as 'in the best situation facing pier and sea'. This scene dates from 1919, when plans for the Blackpool–St Anne's merger came to nothing.

Paddling at St Anne's, c. 1890, when hitching up garments was acceptable. At Lytham in 1799 there were three bathing machines and all were unashamedly lined up together until, 'to maintain order, a House of Correction was built in Douglas Street which had distinct rooms for the punishment of males and females'. No mixed bathing was allowed.

'Louise and Little Robin', 1882. Robin, aged two, is the Robert Howarth on p. 86. Louise Stubbs, a Lytham girl, became a child minder, or 'mother's help' as it was then known, working in Bispham and later for the Howarth family in St Anne's. She married Mr Gillett of Lytham. The studio furniture and Victorian clothing show interesting detail. Robert's mother, who died aged sixty, was a member of the Fielding family.

A St Anne's-on-Sea station porter in front of enamelled, tin-plate advertisements, 1919: 'Finnigans of Deansgate, Manchester, birthday presents', 'Stephens Ink for writers' and 'Jewsbury and Brown Minerals'. A long-serving porter of the time was Charles Sutcliffe. The first stationmaster was Mr Cookson, who lived at 43 St Andrew's Road North.

Outside St Anne's station in the early 1900s. Landaus and covered one-horse carriages wait to escort visitors to their hotels and lodging houses. Some of the boys were happy to carry luggage for a small fee.

The railway station at St Anne's-on-Sea in the 1920s, shown on an embossed, ivy-leaved greetings card published by A.J. Evans. In the 1870s there was a level-crossing by the station door. The rapid growth of the town's population and the influx of visitors meant that the platform had to be enlarged and the level-crossing done away with to cope with the increase in rail traffic.

The lake, with rowing boats and the public baths, was provided by the Fairhaven Estate Co. and became a major attraction. The Shareholders' Annual Meeting at Pollux Gate in 1910 was held during a depression and following a wet summer. However, the chairman, Mr John Rome, said the directors could congratulate themselves on an improved balance sheet.

'Greetings from St Ann's-on-Sea' shows an area of The Crescent within a life belt. In the 1920s these two girls were busy posing for all the Fylde coast resorts, such as Bispham, Cleveleys and Fleetwood. Note how St Anne's has here been spelt incorrectly.

Ashton Gardens (formerly St George's Gardens), 1900, by which time a great change had come over the North and South Promenades. Flowerbeds, paths, rockeries and a waterfall had been constructed, and the gardens were overlooked by fine residences and lodging houses. The main gateway on Clifton Drive was once the entrance to Mr Porritt's building yard.

This view of St Anne's-on-Sea Crescent was on sale as a 'Rapid Photo' in the early 1900s, when bicycles, horses and carts had the road to themselves. In this area there once stood shippons, stables and whitewashed cottages. By 1925 the population of the town had increased to 15,000.

G. Benner and Co., high-class grocers and provision merchants of 38 The Square, St Anne's, made daily motor deliveries during the 1920s in the town and district. Blackboards outside the full shop window offer competitive prices for butter and bacon.

Robert W. Howarth, born on 26 December 1880, worked for a year and ten months at Gill and Read, outfitters, in St Anne's Square opposite Hydro Terrace, before moving to Goodson's of Manchester. He later became manager of Moss Brothers in that city. Long shop hours until 9 p.m. and the old system of 'living in' are reflected in his diary.

A fashionable wedding in St Anne's, 1902. Behind the three girls on the front row are Mr and Mrs W. Howarth, flanked by Walter Scowcroft (born in 1840) and his wife Harriet. Ground-length dresses, elaborate hats and bouquets for the ladies were all evident at the Drive Methodist church ceremony.

This greetings card of paddling at St Anne's-on-Sea, with a fine view of the beach and pier, dates from the early 1900s when messages were written on the front of postcards.

St Anne's tramcar No. 15 rumbles along, advertising Colman's mustard and Dr Lovelace's soap. With only two cyclists and one pedestrian in sight, cycling must have been very pleasant in 1910. An 1893 guide describes Headroomgate Road as 'a capital highway for cyclists'.

This photograph of York Road, taken in the early 1900s when work on it wasn't complete, indicates how useful a horse and cart were for delivering goods and getting about in general. In 1924 W.E. Lord, carrier, was making deliveries to Lytham St Anne's, Ansdell, Fairhaven, Kirkham and Freckleton. (Courtesy of the *Evening Gazette*)

St Anne's Road South, 1889, with Smethurst's, grocers, on the left, showing the quality of building and the excellent use of space. Elijah Hargreaves and W.J. Porritt of Helmshore built some fine houses in the new St Anne's. The Promenade, public gardens and gasworks were constructed in 1875, but shortly afterwards a period of depression set in. By 1886 the pier had been opened and from then on the number of buildings multiplied. The population had reached 6,500 by 1900. Messrs Maxwell and Tuke were responsible for the design and layout of the town. Others who came to build were John Heap, Frank Lomax, W.H. Nutter, Thomas Riley and John Pennington. These men, most of whose families grew up here, may be regarded as pioneers.

Strickland's tobacconists, c. 1892. J. Smith's Glasgow Mixture, Capstan tobacco and cigarettes, and St Bruno with its 'nutty flavour' were all sold at Strickland's, and so were remedies, as the doctor was only called when absolutely necessary. Hair restorers, notably Mr Toole's brand, were stocked for gentlemen customers. Some older ladies were known to smoke tobacco in clay pipes.

Oil lamps of this kind were used a hundred years ago to light farmhouses and cottages in Lytham, Kirkham and the surrounding villages. This one is particularly nostalgic as the rural scene painted below the funnel glows when the lamp is lit. The usual three rooms or 'bays' of a typical cottage would probably house a spinning wheel, winnocks or 'piggins' (milk buckets), presses (cupboards) and a settle.

St Anne's Road West, c. 1921, has so little motorized traffic that people can loiter safely. The van on the left is similar to the mystery delivery van below. If anyone remembers a J.E. Beale & Sons with a vintage delivery van, Lytham Heritage would like to know.

St Anne's jetty. Prior to 1897 there were many fishing smacks and small pleasure boats working from both sides of the jetty. Steamboats took parties for hourly pleasure trips to Lytham, Southport, Liverpool, Fleetwood and Morecambe. *Irene* was owned by the Melling family.

Donkeys on the sands at St Anne's. In 1880 the St Anne's donkeys were owned by a character called Peter 'strong ith'arm' and George Mayes. By the 1890s, when Mr Wykeham Clifton was a familiar figure daily striding the beach, there were twenty bathing machines with attendants, a hand-turned roundabout and four sets of donkeys owned by Betty Candlish, the Whitesides and the Jamesons.

The complete length of St Anne's Pier, with the paddling pool in the foreground. A three-storey, iron extension engineered by Messrs Garlick and Sykes of Preston was built for use by steamer passengers.

This postcard of the Roman Baths, which were 80 yds long and 40 yds wide and opened at St Anne's in 1916, carries Alice's message: 'Dear Edith. It has turned out a beautiful morning again. Dad and I went to the baths before breakfast. It was fine. The water slide was better patronised than the high diving board.'

Renamed Ashton Gardens in 1920, the original St George's Gardens were established in 1875,
the year in which the foundation stone of St Anne's Hotel was laid by Lady Eleanor Cecily
Clifton and her grandson John Talbot Clifton. Mr Porritt built his 'Garden City' round the
gardens, but 1880 saw a slump in the building trade until Messrs Maden and Trickett from
Waterfoot added their strength. From then on the town never looked back and tradesmen
flourished. J.H. Shimwell, chemist, made up physicians' prescriptions. Joseph Hesketh and Sons,
paper-hangers and decorators of Ansdell, were well known for house signs. Janet Osbaldeston
of the Imperial Steam Laundry announced: 'My van will call'. Ladies were invited to see for
themselves the hand-finishing and drying out of doors. Ryan's Noted Ices were sold on the beach
and father could buy the finest threepenny cigar, the Roxella, for 8s. 6d. per box of fifty.

St Anne's Technical School, opened in 1907 with Mr R.H. Irving as headmaster, aimed 'to enable boys and girls just leaving school to obtain vocational knowledge and prepare themselves for the delightful duties of citizenship'. From inception a wide range of courses were available, including City and Guilds London Institute Examinations. The Silver and Bronze Lundie Memorial Medals and Birley Award were competed for. Now part of the Blackpool and Fylde College of Further and Higher Education, only a few interior green and yellow Edwardian 'lily' tiles remain from the days of Councillor J. Whiteside, who laid the foundation stone. The railings were taken for the war effort in the 1940s, a few years before this photograph was taken. (Courtesy of the *Lancashire Evening Post*)

This postcard of Hotel Glendower, 32–4 North Promenade, St Anne's-on-Sea, is dated 1954. 'Having a lovely holiday, Dence likes playing in the sand and paddling', is the message.

The Fountain on Central Promenade became part of the gardens and grotto laid out in the early years of the resort (1908–9) by Henry Gregson, one-time surveyor to the Clifton Estate. Henry wrote a dialect account of how a time capsule was built into the rockery bridge (see p. 98).

In 1959 an area of 20 acres, including Lovers' Lane and an enormous sand hill opposite Lord Ashton's bungalow, was sold to a Blackpool firm of builders' merchants for £4,000, to be developed as Kilgrimol Estate. At 1,000 ft long and 40 ft high the sand hill was said by the locals to be as big as the *Queen Mary*.

The ladies' sitting-room at the Blackburn and District Convalescent Home, 1932. The postmark has the slogan: 'The telephone—a wise investment'. The lady who wrote the card to Uncle Alf was feeling sad. 'I don't think anybody thinks about me. I have not had a line through anybody.'

The rose gardens in Ashton Gardens, 1921. These were laid out in the earliest days (c. 1880) as pleasure and tea gardens, but came up for sale in 1898 (while still known as St George's Gardens). The Lancaster philanthropist Lord Ashton, in order to 'restore harmony to Council', advanced £21,350 for their purchase with a further gift of £4,526, hence the change of name to Ashton.

Rockery bridge, completed on 9 June 1909. The son of William Gregson (a Great Eccleston travelling tailor), Henry Gregson of Grove Cottage who was a Lytham character, designed and laid out the Promenade Gardens. Tom Hornby, a workman, unceremoniously buried a bottle containing coins and copies of the *St Anne's-on-the-Sea* Express. Henry records that both then 'went off for a jug of ale'.

Bamber's Farm, Bamber's Lane, Marton Moss, demolished in the 1920s, was an example of a thatched cottage and outbuildings built in local brick. Ploughs have turned up many ancient tree trunks on Marton Moss which were toppled by the surge of seas hundreds of years ago. From this hard bog oak, villagers carved furniture and ornaments.

The White Church at Fairhaven was built in 1912 and became a notable landmark in the Byzantine architectural style. Luke Walmsley, one of the founding members, designed the two glorious stained-glass windows whose subjects range from Easter Morn through Calvary, The Ascension, Moses descending from Sinai and Scenes from the Life of Jesus to The Apostles Peter and Paul.

ROUGH SEA, ST ANNES-ON-SEA.

St Anne's Pier at high tide. The pier was opened by the Hon. F. Stanley in 1885 (Mr W.H. Nutter was the manager) and became very popular for its musical entertainment. Mr Dallas and his troupe gave open-air concerts for several seasons, followed by Mr Carlton and his pierrots. By 1904 concerts in the New Moorish Pavilion were drawing crowds to be 'capitally entertained'. Wet weather was no longer a problem, as the walls of the pavilion were covered with Opalite and a thousand people could be seated inside.

St Anne's pier head. Horse-drawn landaus bring visitors to the Floral Hall designed by
E. England. For a charge of 1d. Miss Kate Earl and twelve fellow musicians gave lengthy concerts.
Claude Hulbert, Russ Conway and Leslie Henson also performed here.

The Promenade Gardens, monument, bandstand and pier head make this a classic
St Anne's scene, but the boy entrusted with the bassinette and his baby brother seems bored.

To visit the . . .
SCENES OF WRECKS, and the LIFEBOAT MONUMENTS
. . . at St. Annes and Lytham,

GO BY

THE . . .

ELECTRIC CAR

TO

LYTHAM

AND

ST. ANNES.

'Go by the electric tram to Lytham and St Anne's to visit scenes of wrecks and the Lifeboat Monuments' and 'Jump on a car and have a ripping ride to Lytham' are examples of posters that could be seen in the early 1900s. So popular was travelling by tram that for many years it was hoped that a strong transporter bridge would be constructed over the River Ribble on which trams could continue to Southport. Nothing, however, came of the scheme.

The No. 12 tramcar speeding to Lytham. The journey from Blackpool to Lytham through the sand hills was very popular. This photograph taken around 1910 shows the starr hills in all their primitive wildness, at a time when sea holly, sea lavender, thrift and evening primroses grew in abundance and small green lizards darted out in the sunshine. A great gale ('the worst storm in the history of the Fylde', as it was described on 31 October 1927) 'snapped steel bars like matches' and reached its height in St Anne's shortly before midnight. Breaking through the sand hills at North Drive, the tide flooded the street to a depth of 6 ft, producing a vast lake, piling up seaweed and gravel, and flattening the front wall of the Ormerod Convalescent Home. The lights failed at the Lytham St Anne's Tramways Department at Squire's Gate, so the manager sent his son, Kenneth Laing, with a driver to the substation in St Thomas's Road, where their bus became marooned. When tall Kenneth scrambled out the water came up to his neck.

This view of the Promenade and pier head on a summer day illustrates the pleasant, healthy situation of St Anne's. The 1931 *Medical Officer's Report* given by John P. Litt pointed out, 'the many advantages from a health point of view ... sufferers from rheumatism, asthma can live here in comparative comfort, the winters being mild and the summers not unpleasantly hot'.

This multicard of St Anne's shows the sign referring to daily orchestral concerts. Ashton Gardens and the sands were still popular, as well as that flagship of hotels, the Majestic, where many people stayed, including Winston Churchill. This picture postcard was posted two months before the outbreak of the Second World War.

Three

Lytham St Anne's

This Lytham St Anne's 'Sea Breezes and Sunshine' poster, produced by the London, Midland & Scottish Railway Co. in 1930, is now a collector's item.

In 1908 this wagonette with its load of passengers was journeying into history, as motor charabancs were replacing these once-popular conveyances. Trips from St Anne's were made to Wrea Green where parties stopped at The Grapes for buttered scones, and strawberries and cream.

Green Drive Lodge, at one of the entrances to Lytham Hall Park, and the tree-lined Green Drive were enjoyed by visitors in the 1920s as a change from crowded North Beach, in the days when the sands were golden and free from spartina grass.

Haymaking at Bolton House Farm, c. 1926. At this time farming was undergoing many changes. The old method of piling hay onto a cart was replaced by mechanical reapers and binders. 'Folmarts' or 'foul martins' (polecats), with their strong smell, were sometimes disturbed in the haystacking process, and hares were plentiful. The Clifton Cup and the Lytham Cup used to be competed for at the Ridgeway Coursing Club's Lytham meeting.

Isaac Ball with nine workmen. The Ball brothers came from Banks in 1870, Isaac settling at
Wharles where he built up a good business. They repaired steam engines and traction engines,
receiving orders from all over Lancashire. Their threshing outfits were hired by Lytham St
Anne's farms and Isaac (with the bushy moustache) helped with the harvest.

Mauretania, the Burrell 3297 traction engine, early 1900s. This was one of Isaac Ball's thirty-five machines available for hire. Baling was a noisy, dusty process, with chaff being collected in the large sacks. Farmers generally helped each other. At the farm at North Houses, Headroomgate, the first female child in the new town of St Anne's, Maggie Hargreaves, daughter of the farmer Robert Hargreaves, was born. 'Daddy' Whiteside's farm and Twiggy Hill Farm were near the picturesque cottages of Twiggy Lane and looked out across the Common, which is now a built-up area.

Two heavy horses, with Mr Cowperthwaite of Higher Fall Farm, Clifton Road, ploughing at Little Marton, 1918. By 1842 the high cost of building Fleetwood and the Preston & Wyre Railway had forced Sir Peter Hesketh Fleetwood to sell parcels of his land, including this area, to Thomas Clifton of Lytham Hall. The manor of Marton had been acquired by Cuthbert Clifton in the seventeenth century.

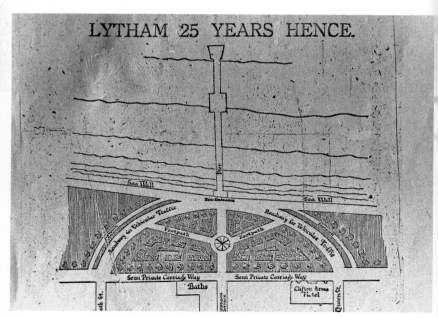

LYTHAM 25 YEARS HENCE.

The New Town Hall, previously the Southdown Hydro, was purchased in 1925. On a very wet day, 1 May 1922, the granting of the Charter was celebrated with six aldermen and eighteen town councillors in attendance. Crowds assembled in front of the shops and clock tower on St Anne's Road West to hear the official proclamation read out. For this historic day 'a grand programme of ceremonial and festivity went forward, undeterred by the steady downpour of rain'. The full programme, except for the children's sports, was carried out. The *St Anne's-on-the-Sea Express* placed on record this event of such historic interest to the new borough with reports, photographs and special articles. Among many speeches, Councillor Chadwick remarked that he hoped Lytham St Anne's would become one of the most noted boroughs in the land.

Opposite below: The *Lytham St Anne's Express* of 11 November 1926. In this year Mr John Crompton designed an 'improved' Lytham, Ansdell and Fairhaven. Although the design never got beyond the drawing board, it can be seen that he envisaged a tree-sheltered, well-laid-out garden between the baths and the pier.

Councillor C.F. Critchley, JP, was the first elected mayor of the new Borough of Lytham St Anne's, which came into being at the first meeting of the new Town Council on 9 November 1922. Of the eighteen town councillors, half represented Lytham and half St Anne's. In its early days St Anne's was governed by a Local Board which was superceded by an Urban District Council.

The Charter Day official celebration, 1 May 1922, when the dignitaries gathered to proclaim the union of Lytham with St Anne's-on-Sea. On the right of the group on the platform are J. Talbot Clifton, Lord of the Manor, and his son and heir, Harry de Vere Clifton.

Members and officials of St Anne's Council, 1922. Seated, left to right: Councillor C.F. Critchley, JP (Chairman and Charter Mayor), Councillor R. Leigh (Vice-Chairman). Middle row: Mr H.J. Carmont, Mr T. Bradley (Charter Town Clerk), Councillor J. Watts, Councillor H.W. Laing (General Manager, Tramways), Councillor J.H. Taylor, Councillor J.W Hallam, Councillor G.R. Eyre, Mr G. Lawson (Surveyor).

St Anne's War Memorial Hospital had previously been the home of Thomas Bannister, when it was known as Banastre Holme. The Trustees paid £10,000 for it in 1920 but extensive alterations from plans prepared by James Miller of Glasgow added to the final cost.

The St Anne's War Memorial Hospital was opened on Charter Day, 1922, by the Earl of Derby (centre). Forty-five rooms, an operating theatre, staff accommodation and central hot-water heating added to the initial cost, but outwardly the building appeared little changed except for a glass veranda.

The Square, St Anne's, in the 1940s retains the familiar landmarks of the clock tower, wide street and quality shops for which it became reowned. The greatest change is the increase in traffic.

Seafield Preparation School, photographed in 1890, was one of a number of educational establishments set near the healthy sand hills. During the summer holidays of 1892 five Lytham schoolboys, Harold, Davis, Lionel, Edgar and Frank, put into verse a sailing adventure which commenced thus:

> We sailed from St Anne's jetty against a heavy breeze
> Passing St Anne's lighthouse, riding heavy seas.
> We sailed by Lytham Windmill
> Then on to Warton came.
> Turning the Naze at Freckleton,
> We had a risky game.

The putting green at St Anne's was another attraction for visitors. All along the Fylde coast, greens were being laid out in the 1930s, and Lytham St Anne's, one of the country's most famous golfing names, was not going to be left out.

These three bottles are from (left to right) the Talbot Hotel, where Mr Salthouse was licensee, H.H. Gourlay, pharmaceutical chemists, and the Ship and Royal Hotel, where T. Windebank was landlord.

These cottages in Church Road, St Anne's, originally had thatched roofs. It was here that the Eastham, Hall and Cartmell families lived. In 1872 Lady Eleanor Cecily Clifton had cottages built in Headroomgate Road of which the first tenant was Alexander Eaves.

Watchwood Lodge, Ballam Road, stood at one of the entrances to the thickly wooded Lytham Hall Park, which extended for some 616 acres. On certain days in the early 1900s the grounds were open to visitors by a ticket obtainable from the Estate Office near the Market Hall. The 'Invalid's Walk' was especially popular.

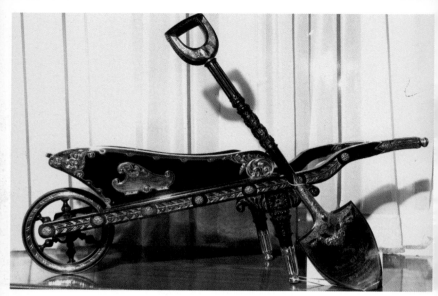

The silver and ebony spade and wheelbarrow used by William J. Porritt on 18 August 1892, when he cut the first sod of St Anne's main drainage scheme. They were presented to Chairman Gabriel Harrison in 1970 when the Amalgamated & Property Co. Ltd purchased the share capital of the St Anne's-on-Sea Land & Building Co. Ltd.

The Bradford District Rechabites' Memorial Home on South Drive is just one example of fine premises in St Anne's bought to accommodate people from the inland industrial towns during well-earned holidays.

The first Ladies' Golf Championship at St Anne's, May 1893. Lady Margaret Scott (back row, second from right) was the winner. 'Some of the finest golf links in the country' drew visitors to the South Fylde in the early 1900s. At Lytham and St Anne's Links visitors were allowed to play the eighteen holes for 10s. per week or 2s. 6d. per day, and there was also the Old Links Golf Club. Indeed, the hotels and boarding houses were heavily patronised by golfers, and today's Royal Lytham golf tournaments still attract many overseas visitors and players. The ladies on this notable occasion came from all over Britain. The Royal Lytham and St Anne's Golf Club originated from a meeting held in the St Anne's Hotel in February 1886. Nineteen founder members headed by Alexander Doleman, who used to practise golf by himself in the sand hills, settled on one guinea per annum as a suitable subscription. A caddie was paid 9d. for his services over eighteen holes. The secretary was J. Talbot Fair, and the first captain Sidney A. Herman, presenter of the Herman Cigar Box trophy. The course was reached by crossing the railway line at St Anne's station and climbing over a fence. Opened officially by the Marquis of Lorne in 1898, Lytham and St Anne's became 'Royal' in 1926, the year of the first Open won by Bobby Jones, who returned in 1944.

The new road to Lytham (arrowed in this photograph) after its opening in 1926. The track on the left traversed Freckleton Marsh, where there was one of the last remaining toll bars in the country. Mr Stanley Brown of East Beach, Lytham, recalls riding along this road in 1926 on his new bicycle, a reward for having won a scholarship to King Edward VII School. (Courtesy of the *Lancashire Evening Post*)

The sea flooding in October 1927 was the worst in living memory on the Fylde coast. At Fleetwood it engulfed the town, and at Lytham it took a huge bite out of the Promenade. Townspeople and workers survey the damage in this *Evening Gazette* photograph, with the windmill and lifeboat house in the background. A scheme to strengthen the sand hills, natural sea defences opposite King Edward VII School, by replanting marram grass suffered from vandalism in March 1983. In the great storms between 1857 and 1900 rescues by the Lytham lifeboat totalled 185 lives. A profitable venture for the lifeboatmen was salvaging the vessel *Chiltonford*, a four-masted Glasgow barque found drifting derelict in the Ribble Estuary on 21 December 1900. Its crew had abandoned ship and boarded the tugboat *Stormcock*. The Lytham crew managed to move the *Chiltonford* off the Horsebank and each member received £170 in salvage money. Two lifeboatmen bought horses and carts and set up fish rounds, Tom Hardman's family carrying on his round for many years.

This fountain, originally in Market Square, Lytham, but later moved to near Lytham new station, was erected by Lady Clifton in memory of her husband John Talbot, who died in Hamman Rhea, Algiers, on 16 April 1882. The stone inscription around it reads, ' 'Tis well 'tis something we may stand, where he in English earth is laid.' At each of the four corners are three carved wooden pillars.

'Off for a ride at St Anne's-on-Sea', 1920. This was a great favourite with parents to take home when the holiday ended. The photographer was on the sands all season to capture groups like this.

'Greetings from St Anne's-on-Sea' is printed on the reverse of this postcard from 1930, showing the St Anne's Hotel which was conveniently placed near the railway station. The first St Anne's golf course was alongside, and inside the hotel members had the use of a golf room with clubs mounted on the wall.

Mrs Annie Rigby, the first Lytham Rose Queen in 1894 when she was 13½-year-old Annie Johnson, greets another queen seventy-five years later. Once again she had ridden through the streets of Lytham but in 1894 it was in an open, lavishly decorated phaeton carriage, at a time when there was no electricity and ladies wore skirts that swept the ground. The 1969 Rose Queen was Jill Rossall. 'Queen Annie' was still watching Club Day processions when she was aged 94. As Annie Johnson she represented St Cuthbert's church.

St Anne's Library, 1940s, with the technical college alongside. The town took its name from the church, erected in 1872 for the benefit of the farmers of Heyhouses. St Anne's soon became known as 'The Opal of the West'. It acquired its library, like that of nearby Blackpool, through the generosity of the philanthropist Andrew Carnegie.

The War Memorial, Ashton Gardens, St Anne's-on-Sea, 1930. The bronze frieze encircling the memorial bears the names of Lytham St Anne's men who were sacrificed in the two World Wars.

Their Majesties King George VI and Queen Elizabeth met civic leaders on 17 May 1938. A colossal arch at Squire's Gate bore the word 'Welcome', and cheering thousands lined the route. Here the royal party is leaving the dais outside St Anne's Pier with Lord Derby and the Mayor of Lytham St Anne's, Lady Edge.

Lowther Gardens, Lytham, covering 12 acres, were presented to the council by Squire Clifton when military bands were still a seaside feature. In this five-scene card, posted in 1925, are the pavilion, tennis courts, rose gardens, bowling green and lawns. By 1926 a ladies' orchestra played in the Lowther Pavilion.

Lytham St Anne's schoolboys' cricket team, 1930s. Back row: Eastwood, Dawson, -?-, Jackson. Front row: Carter, Wilkes, Cartmell, Hoyle. St Anne's Cricket Club, founded in 1888, won the Alhambra Shield Competition in 1902. As early as 1870 cricket was played at Headroomgate Road on the site of the parish rooms.

Lytham Windmill, c. 1930, when it was a café. There was a windmill on this site in 1190 when Richard Fitz Roger gave the land to the Benedictine monks at Durham. The sails of the mill were shortened in 1909 following a tragedy. A Manchester schoolboy, one of a party, caught hold of a sail and was whirled aloft. As he reached the highest point he released his grip and fell to the ground, whereupon he was killed instantly. Since then the mill has served many purposes, Ye Olde Windmill Café being one.

The old goods yard, Lytham, 1940. The independent Blackpool & Lytham Railway was established under an Act of 1861. The route was to pass South Shore and Lytham new station to the junction with the Kirkham and Lytham branch. On 6 April 1863 the line was opened for traffic and eight years later was absorbed as part of the Preston & Wyre system. Another important railway branch constructed by the old Preston & Wyre Co. commenced near Kirkham and terminated at the old railway station, Lytham, which was later used for goods traffic only, as here.

Hauled by locomotive No. 10607, the Lytham local train passes Gillett's Crossing, so called because it was near Gillett's Farm. Sparks from railway engines could set surrounding land on fire, which resulted in correspondence between the Fairs, father and son, agents to the Cliftons, and the railway company about damage done to trees and crops. Such correspondence often led to litigation by landowners in the Fylde. (Courtesy of the *Evening Gazette*)

The St Anne's Pier Orchestra, 1930, with its conductress Clarice Dunnington. George Lord of St Anne's Road South and the Pier Studio took this photograph, one of a variety on sale to visitors. In 1910 Kate Earl and twelve lady musicians gave similiar concerts.

Freckleton Band on Lytham Club Day. Galas and fêtes in Fylde were attended by other bands besides that of Lytham. Kirkham and St Anne's also had brass bands that were called upon for civic functions.

This Lytham St Anne's tram, No. 9, advertising Wee Georgie Wood at The Palace, Blackpool, is still in service. An annual occasion, when vintage trams run from Squire's Gate to Fleetwood, has proved very popular.

The Promenade, Lytham, on a clear day in 1948, with Southport and the North Wales hills visible in the distance. 'Save your waste paper for salvage', instructs the franking on the reverse of this postcard. The war was over but it was still a time of austerity. 'The mill is being restored and put in working order,' writes brother Bob from Eden Avenue, Lytham.

Clearing sand from the tram track, 1928. Clifton Drive, laid out by Colonel John T. Clifton, ran from Lytham Hall to Squire's Gate. In 1873 it was nothing more than a waste of sand hills and marram grass. Gale-force winds and stormy seas always created the problem of sand clogging the tram track. Gales in the early 1900s sucked out the plate-glass windows of four shops in the centre of St Anne's and snapped the big flagstaff at Royal Lytham and St Anne's Golf Club. The *Blackpool Gazette and Herald* and *Fylde News and Advertiser* issued special storm picture editions, price 1d., showing the trail of destruction.

A wartime Christmas card of Lytham front. This linocut was designed by Stanley Brown of East Beach, Lytham, in 1940, the blockade year when almost everything was in short supply. Lytham's famous trademark, the white 'windy milne', was a happy thought.

A street party in St Anne's, 1945, celebrating the end of the Second World War. An enemy plane hit houses in Church Road, St Anne's, on 29 September 1941, killing one person and injuring nine. Houses were also damaged in Kirkham where two people were killed and seven injured, but on the whole the area was considered a safe haven.

The building in 1882 of Lytham Baths and Assembly Rooms, situated midway between the Clifton Arms and Neptune Hotel, coincided with the linking of Blackpool and Lytham by coast railway, a scheme devised by John Talbot Clifton, T. Langton Birley and Charles Birley of Kirkham. Brick-built with stone dressings, the Baths and Assembly Rooms offered private and public swimming baths, dressing rooms, newspaper and general reading rooms, and a concert hall where balls were held. This fine building replaced the original one in 1927, but much of it has been given over to flats. The Neptune, situated on the corner of Bath Street, has changed its name to the Queen's Hotel. (Courtesy of the *Lancashire Evening Post*)

Opposite below: Freddie Johnson (right) with his father, Bandmaster Charlie William Johnson of the Lytham Volunteer Band. Of many anecdotes recalled by Freddie, one tells of the band playing by Fairhaven Lake. In the middle of The Desert Song a sudden mighty wind toppled the music stands and swept away the scores.

In 1882 Lytham Baths and Assembly Rooms were provided to replace a billiard hall and reading room. The venture failed financially, but Mr Clifton supported it until 1920 when the local council took over. Many Lytham Rose Queens were crowned on the steps on the right.

Lytham Pier under snow, 1940. The pier was very popular with visitors each summer, but in 1928 it was almost entirely destroyed by fire, one of a number of pier fires along the Lancashire coast. It became such a rusting eyesore that a campaign was waged for its removal. After a nine-hour public inquiry the decision was approved and the pier demolished in 1960. The opening of Lytham Pier on Easter Monday 1865 had been one of the town's great days. Special trains were run from Preston to bring in the crowds. The Friendly Societies congregated in Market Place and headed for the new pier, led by the band of the Third Lancashire Militia. The Lytham Volunteers formed a guard of honour and Mrs Clifton emerged from the Assembly Rooms to complete the ceremony.

The quaint charm of a seaside resort out of season is expressed in this *Lancashire Evening Post* photograph of Lytham Pier in 1956, with its 'Jugs of Tea' sign reminiscent of fifty years before: 'Ice cream—wafers, cornets, fruit sundaes, pineapple, strawberry, peach, etc., minerals, ice drinks, tea bar'. To 'walk for exercise' cost only 2d., but it was 4d. extra for a bassinette and 6d. for a bath chair. A 1909 report on Lytham Pier by Dr Poole tells us that this 900 ft iron structure, 'the popular centre of the Promenaders' joys, had a splendid pavilion in the midst of the waves'. Drama, light opera and musical comedy performances were held regularly, and at midsummer one of the finest musical festivals in the North of England was held, attracting top performers.

The library interior at King Edward VII School. Such interesting glimpses into the past were usually captured by magnesium flash, hence the term 'flashlight photography'. In the 1920s Mr Hedges and Mr Ellis Wolstenholme were local exponents of the technique.

An LMS goods train leaving Lytham St Anne's, 1930s. In 1843 a local sailor said of the railway locomotive, 'Nothing manly about it. Coming incinivating on its belly like a thundering long snake with a pipe in its mouth!'

The result of Save the Soldier Week. Announcing the final figure of £767,229 achieved by Lytham St Anne's, the mayor, Councillor J.R. Taylor, said, 'I give you thanks from the bottom of my heart.' Walter Heap is next to him and Councillor Lindsay Dobson first on the left.

Some of the 2,250 forces parcels despatched from the Mayoress's Comforts Fund, 10 December 1943. These contained toothbrushes, toothpaste, razor blades, socks, postal orders and cigarettes. Left to right: Mrs H. Moulden, Mrs C.H. Wilkes, Mrs C.S. Urwin, Miss Lees, Mrs V.W. Pilkington, Mrs R. Housley, Mrs R. Austin.

Lytham police station, situated on the corner of North Clifton Street and Bannister Street, is well sandbagged, as were all the constabularies during the Second World War. Two police houses were also provided. In the days of the 'bobby on the beat' there appears to have been little crime in Lytham St Anne's, although the nation was shocked early this century by a murder in the sand hills. An itinerant chair mender who got drunk and became aggressive was sent to prison in 1922. In 1843 Constable Cragg arrested two boys who had stolen a coil of rope. They were 'committed to the House of Correction at Preston for trial at the ensuing sessions'. Most crime was of a petty nature, but the details of the murder caused a sensation through the country. A local man murdered a young woman—a former beauty queen—from Yorkshire, having previously insured her life for a large sum of money.

Britannia and friends, after staging a pageant to aid the war effort, are congratulated by J.H. Taylor, JP. Forty-three years a St Anne's resident, he was chairman of St Anne's District Council from 1913 to 1915, a governor of Lytham Charities and chairman of the governors of St Anne's Memorial Hospital.

By the 1930s Lytham St Anne's had the 'fabulous' Lytham Picture Palace in Clifton Street, next to T.A. Brummett's, newsagent, and near the Lytham Creamery. On certain nights this Blackpool Tower Co. cinema featured a good violinist playing in the pit.

A practice launch of the Lytham lifeboat, 1936. Monday 15 June 1885 saw the ceremonial launching of lifeboat *Laura Janet* by Mrs Chadwick and the opening of St Anne's Pier. The lifeboats of Lytham, Blackpool, Southport and St Anne's lined up before thirty thousand visitors. Brass bands, fluttering flags and bunting marked the occasion. Giving an address in St Anne's-on-Sea on the history of lifeboats in 1890, Revd W. Elstud said, 'Each year on this stretch of British seaboard an average of 700 lives are lost.' When the *Ocean Monarch* caught fire in sight of land in August 1848, many would-be emigrants jumped into the sea to escape the flames. Bodies were washed up all along the Fylde coast. At Lytham Mr and Mrs Murtophy, baby Jane Murtophy and two boys of sixteen were buried in St Cuthbert's churchyard.

Along Clifton Drive on 27 January 1954, lorries were used as snowploughs after the heaviest fall of snow for many years. In an area unused to frost and snow, this was a rare occasion in contrast with what Gabriel Harrison described as 'the rage of sand'. This stretch is now the area specially set aside as a nature reserve. Fairhaven Golf Club, established in 1895, was laid out over similar terrain. Its clubhouse became the Fairhaven Lake Café and golfers had a good view of trams thundering between Blackpool and Lytham St Anne's. (Courtesy of the *Lancashire Evening Post*)

The British Legion Band, among its many ups and downs, lost all of its instruments in a fire but managed to reorganize in the 1950s. As it met at the British Legion premises it assumed that name. Behind the drum is the bandmaster, Charlie Johnson.

Jill Dee of Lytham Heritage Group holds what may be a carriage candle lamp, unearthed about ten years ago from Lytham Hall grounds. It may have adorned a gig or landau belonging to one of Lytham's squires, or it could have been a pilot's lamp as it is fitted with green glass on one side and red on the other.

From the lone sand yacht of Peter Hesketh in 1830 has grown the Fylde International Sand Yacht Club which began in 1951 and which hosts national and international competitions. In 1953 Richard Denning broke the British and world speed records in the sand yacht *Coronation* II. A speed of 70 mph has been reached, but blowing sand sometimes interferes with the recording equipment. (Courtesy *Lancashire Magazine*)

The Hotel Majestic, a falling giant, with an exit sign hanging over a gaping hole on 3 January 1975 as its demolition continues. It was a big undertaking to raze such a vast building. Luxury flats and a modern tavern were erected on this spacious seafront site facing the Town Hall. Little remains of the hotel other than the gateposts marked IH, indicating Imperial Hydro, the former name of the Majestic. (Courtesy of the *Lancashire Evening Post*)

This view of the frontage of the Hotel Majestic and the steps leading to its garden was a favourite postcard to send home when on holiday. 'All the nobs stay here', said one greetings card in the 1930s.

Our Lady Star of the Sea, photographed in 1934 but opened in June 1890. The steamyacht *Flora*, dedicated under the protection of Mary, Star of the Sea, was owned by the Duchess of Norfolk, whose influence extended to St Anne's and Carleton.

On Easter Sunday 1935, St Anne's pier concourse had a full complement of automobiles, charabancs and a motor bus, with visitors out in force on a popular holiday in the days when there was still relatively little motor traffic. It is interesting to see just one horse and rider where fifty years before there would have been many more and no motor vehicles at all. St Anne's Pier was severely damaged by fire in 1974 when the Floral Hall extension was gutted. Another fire broke out on 24 July 1982, possibly caused by mischievous children. Bingo players at the end of the pier were unaware of what had happened and forty people had to be hurried to safety. Fire officer Tony Fraser and his men were hindered by the presence of holiday-makers. Fire distorted the girders and, as the structure went 50 ft down into the sand, complete removal was impossible. The brothers Webb, owners of the Dalmeny Hotel, bought the pier and Fylde Demolition took six weeks to complete the work. Refurbishment of the pier head and the remaining structure followed. (Courtesy of the *Evening Gazette*)

St Anne's Boating Pool, 1934. Sand from the beach was used in the construction of the pool. Fairhaven Marine Lake was formed between two stanners/pebble ridges. (Courtesy of the *Evening Gazette*)

The Majestic Celebrity Orchestra directed by Gerald Bright, photographed in 1926, played at the Hotel Majestic. In early broadcasting days they 'went on the air' three times a week. When their season ended, Harold Sandler, brother of violinist Albert, followed Geraldo and his Orchestra. 'Geraldo' was the name adopted by Gerald Bright and under which he achieved fame.

Queen Mary School was opened in 1929 on the area that had once been Fairhaven golf links. This photograph is of the fifth form in 1951. Back row, left to right: Audrey Buxton, Joan Wilkinson, Mavis Hardman, Adrienne Harker, Mary Spencer, Audrey Taylor, Nancy Norris, Doreen Marland, Barbara Fitton, Joyce Wyles, Delia Duke, Barbara Entwhistle, Adrienne Wilding, Jean Smithies, Esther Rigby. Middle row: Constance Morrissey, Dorothy Jackson, Kathleen Hilton, Valerie Horridge, Wendy Miller, Margo Munro, Hilary Smith, Nancy Nelson. Front row: Hilary Astell, Audrey Eaborn, Rhona Taylor, -?-, Miss Crawshaw, Janet Ward, Helen Aslam, Margaret Astell, Hazel Burgoyne.

All that remained of Mother Fisher's Cottage, Church Slack, by 1958. The ancient hamlet, with its blowing sands and legend of church bells ringing from the villages buried under the sea, was inevitably in its turn swallowed up by the demand for golf courses.

A panoramic view of Lytham as seen from the shore, photographed in the 1950s by Stanley Brown of Lytham.

Riversleigh, a Lytham mansion photographed in 1950, was the residence of Major Booth and later Mr Sadler, engineer of Lytham Docks. Serving as a home for elderly retired clergymen and their dependants, and refurbished about this time, it was renamed Fosbrook House after Archdeacon Fosbrook who ministered for many years in Lytham. In front of Riversleigh, tree-lined boulevards (Willows Avenue, Riversleigh Avenue, etc.) were built on what were once open fields, with Willows Avenue being the first to be laid out. (Courtesy of the *Lancashire Evening Post*)

Reopening of the bandstand, St Anne's Promenade, July 1982. This Victorian gem was restored after twenty years through the efforts of David and Michael Webb, owners of the Dalmeny Hotel and the pier. In front of three hundred visitors, Freckleton Prize Band started a new era of Sunday afternoon concerts. When the demand for military bands playing at the seaside declined, the bandstand was partly glassed in and served as a shelter. It was also suggested that it should be made into a skating rink, but this was not allowed. The final result of the restoration shown in this *Evening Gazette* photograph is a pleasure to behold. 'Congratulations and celebrations' plays the band, and these were well earned.

This King Edward VII School Old Boys' Reunion celebrated the school's fiftieth birthday in 1958. The group includes Stuart Cartmell (centre) who was one of the original intake in 1908. In 1911 the first *Kestrel* magazine appeared. At this reunion Leslie 'Gussy' Shaw, who left in 1915, reminded the others, 'What school at one time could have three masters named Snowball, Varnish and Pickles?'—King Edward VII had. An endowed public school open to boys aged 10 to 18, the new buildings in 1910 comprised: the 'Big School', 90 ft by 40 ft; ten classrooms; two science laboratories with lecture room; art room; carpenter's shop; library, and a dining hall which could accommodate 150 boys. The fees were £12 per annum.

The Lytham St Anne's horse trough, engraved 'Be Ye Merciful', was very busy in the days when horses and donkeys had to be watered. Considered redundant by the time of this photograph in February 1974, it had reached toppling stage and was being levered out by workmen. In the background are houses built by Mr Porritt which when erected looked immediately onto the sand dunes. In the early 1870s and '80s residents could hear the sound of the sea. (Courtesy of the *Evening Gazette*)

Morris dancing at galas and Club Days in South Fylde has been a long-standing tradition. The Garstang Morris Dancers, who attended most Club Days, photographed after the Calder Vale procession in 1990, are keeping up the custom. Morris batons may alter, but the charm of enthusiastic little girls continues down the years. The traditional costume was all white, with very full dresses, stockings and frilly hats which appear to have been modelled on the Fylde sunbonnet. (Courtesy of the *Garstang Courier*)

Fête Queen Doreen Marsden, on her way to the throne after her coronation, is followed by
Margot Illingworth, the retiring queen, and Jean Fielden, Lytham Rose Queen,
28 August 1954. In the background is the Hotel Majestic, an imposing building which has now
been replaced by flats. (Courtesy of the *Evening Gazette*)

Salt refining was carried out near Lytham Pool. A twelfth-century charter refers to John le Saltwaller. Saltwellers still practised their trade in 1772. In the large tract of land known as Lytham Moss, lead-lined vessels used in the process have been unearthed, preserved by the acid peat soil like the bog oak tree trunks.

Lytham Dockyard, c. 1950. Owing to the shifting, dangerous sandbanks in the River Ribble, large ships had originally to discharge cargoes such as corn at Lytham Pool into lighters which then sailed on to Preston Marsh. At the north end of Lytham Pool was a small graving dock where vessels were built and repaired.

Lytham station, April 1958, displays some interesting vintage posters: Lancaster and Barrow 5s. 6d. and 11s. 6d; Chester and Llandudno 8s. 6d. and 15s. 6d.—these were the days of cheap and frequent trips. The original Preston & Wyre station became a goods depot for coal trucks, and livestock was dealt with at Ansdell. The Lytham St Anne's Civic Society hoped to set up three massive blocks of stone, once part of the façade of old Lytham station, in the Woodland Walk between the skew bridge at Ansdell and the present Lytham station, a popular walk officially opened in 1985 by the Duke of Edinburgh. Ten years earlier Blackpool Corporation had bought part of the fluted columns of the façade for £700, but the cost of the proposed scheme to form these into a triumphal arch was prohibitive, so the stones were left to lie. (Courtesy of the *Lancashire Evening Post*)

Acknowledgements

I am especially indebted to: Stanley Brown of East Beach, Lytham, Syd Hardman of Lytham Heritage Group, Freddie Johnson of Freckleton, Tony Nickson of Royal Lytham and St Anne's Golf Club, Miss B. Rigby of Church Road, Lytham, Arnold Sumner, antique dealer of St Anne's and Mr Jonathan Taylor of J.R. Taylor, St Anne's, for their courtesy and generosity in giving me their time, and to the *Chats* of David Greaves, a charming booklet printed in Pleasant Street, Lytham, in 1925.

Additionally I am grateful to the following for providing old photographs or personal information: Mrs J.R. Barron, Tom Betley, Braithwaite Manor Restaurant, Harold Bridges, Mrs K. Briggs, Alan Burgess, Stanley Butterworth, Rachel Cartmell, Lillias 'Sandy' Cooper, Anthony Coppin, Jill Dee, the late Kathleen Eyre, Sylvia Fenner, Arthur Firth, antique dealer, Robert Gibson, John Gornall, Ken Hall, Lancashire County Archivist, Mr W. Heap, J.C. Hilton Esq., Lord of the Manor of Lytham, K. Hall Houghton, King Edward VII School, *Lancashire Evening Post*, Lancashire Library, St Anne's, Lancashire Museums, Lancashire Record Office, Richard Lancaster, Mrs E. Lougha, Lytham Heritage Group, *Lytham St Anne's Express*, Alex Maitland, Eric Mills, Eileen Norris, Mr D. Owen, Mr R. Pomfret, Queen Mary School, Robinson's Antiques, Ron Severs, P.K. Sharman, Mrs R. Simpson, Derek B. Timms, Rachel Tumblick, Philip Welsh, *West Lancashire Evening Gazette*.

Finally I wish to thank Robert Silverwood and the staff of the Lowther Café, Lytham St Anne's, who sustained us with good, piping-hot meals in the depths   of winter.